To Love
To Share
To Serve

Challenges to A Religious

L. Patrick Carroll, S.J.

THE LITURGICAL PRESS

Collegeville
Minnesota

Dedication

To Linda who constantly encouraged me to write this,
To Katherine Marie who provided at least half
  the ideas,
And to the Jesuits who have lived with me
  while I sort things out,
In deep and lasting gratitude.

First printing, 1979
Second printing, 1980
Third printing, 1981
Fourth printing, 1981
Fifth printing, 1981
Sixth printing, 1982
Seventh printing, 1983

Nihil obstat: Joseph C. Kremer, S.T.L., *Censor deputatus, Imprimatur*: ☩ George H. Speltz, D.D., Bishop of St. Cloud, February 8, 1979.
Printed in the United States of America. ISBN 0-8146-1029-3.

Contents

Introduction

Distance, new perspectives, altered angles assist any effort to understand. When we see our valleys from a different mountain, their beauty shines in new and unsuspected ways. I have been a religious for almost a quarter-century, prayed, studied, thought, tried to understand the mystery I am busy living. From 1970–1977 I was superior of a group of religious men, forced to deepen my own convictions and share them with my community in ways that brought us, together, more fully to life. Often my judgements were more intuitive than informed, more instinct than conviction. Religious life for individuals was and is changing and the perimeters of that life were less certain, more tentative. Many half-formed theories about our need to move from here to there wandered within my mind or heart. I led hesitantly because I walked hesitantly.

From June 1977 to February 1978, I lived and worked with religious in Lesotho, a small, black, independent country in Southern Africa. Lesotho is geographically as far from the northwestern United States as one can get. As a heavily Catholic country, with growing numbers of religious facing many of the same questions and challenges as we, it becomes almost a near neighbor. The ability to see the same things in new light,

1

the chance to read, think, pray in a new setting, the opportunity to present the same kind of material to different people helped to solidify my own convictions about the project that is mine, and yet is ours.

The pages that follow indicate some of the things that moved from instinct to some degree of conviction in my own understanding, things that have been helpful to me as a religious, and may be to you.

There are many excellent books on religious life available already. I have been helped or challenged by many of them. But as I borrowed or rejected other's material, I began to see some things that seemed distinctly my own, however derivative from others. I do not try here to detail everything that is important about religious life but only to indicate single, almost random reflections on areas that seem neglected in other treatments. Consequently, there is much I do not touch. My hope is that what I do touch on seems as significant to you as it does to me if we are to become witnesses again to an alternate Christian lifestyle both supporting and challenging those who share the Church and the much wider world with us.

I also have a newly growing conviction that much of what we read seems written by experts telling us ways in which we can "shape up" and become like them. My aim is less lofty. I would like to chat with you about our common aims and aspirations as they appear to me today. I am convinced of the importance of what I say, but I may be quite wrong and whether wrong or not I am sure that I will change tomorrow as other things become more important. In other words, I want to speak to you as friends on a journey together, tell you my version of the ancient tale. I am not an expert, not, perhaps, a deeply spiritual man. I am honestly trying to let God love me into becoming one. Join me on the journey.

· 1 ·

Religious Life: A Project

It began just two hours after my ordination to the priesthood. I was in a motel room with my family and other friends when the telephone rang, the first of a million phone calls to "Father" Carroll. A friend asked to speak to me, asked if I would hear his confession, said he had waited two years for me to be ordained —would I help him? I said the first of many yeses and then turned to another priest in the room to ask the formula for absolution, which I had not yet learned.

The confession was long, painful, hopefully healing. I did not know the formula for absolution, so read it over his bowed head. More importantly, I did not know how to convey God's healing, loving forgiveness. I would have to learn that. I had been called to be a priest. I was not yet one, no matter how valid the ceremony of a few hours earlier. This experience clarified for me what I had theoretically suspected, the vocational character of any religious event. The sacraments, and every other element of our Christian lives, are not accomplished facts, finishing something, but vocations, calls beginning something.

When I was ordained I was invited by the Lord into a new relationship with him and with his people. I was not yet a priest, a mediator between God and man, a celebrator of the paschal mysteries, a leader of prayer, a healer, reconciler, prophet, and all those things the books glibly say a priest is. I was called to become one.

This notion has helped me struggle through the past eleven years, and I think, by passing it on, I have helped others to struggle also. It seems so obvious. Sacraments are not the end of an event, but the beginning, the invitation—not finished and accomplished facts, but vocations. The same is true of religious life and each of the vows.

When a child is baptized he does not immediately "put on the Lord Jesus," so that "now he lives no longer himself, but Christ lives in him." He is called to begin to do that with the help of his family and the various communities of which he will be a part.

I have never met a married couple who, on the day of their marriage, could honestly say that they were two in one flesh. In fact, marriage as a sacrament calls people to mirror to a community the faithful love of God towards his people, a love that abides through health and sickness, poverty and wealth, good times and bad. This cannot be done except over time. A marriage *becomes* sacramental: a sign to the rest of the community that God's love lives in this couple and that permanence is possible. What the ceremony does, provided both parties know (which they too rarely do) and accept that call, is to celebrate the invitation God gives to two people to be signs of his life. It is a call, not a fact.

I have received the Eucharist many times, but, somehow, the life of Jesus is not yet fully in me. His blood does not totally fill my veins, his flesh my bones. I am called to this in each Mass. So the most important words of the Eucharistic celebration are not "This is my body, . . .my blood," but "Go in peace to love and serve the Lord." The Mass is a vocation to be lived out in the market place.

The point of all this is to indicate that the same is true of religious life and the vows, which are the traditional formulation of that life. Poverty, chastity, obedience (even the added inference—"within community") bespeak vocation, call, not fact accomplished at the time of their pronouncement.

Let me step back a moment and suggest why I think this is true. Religious vows are not separate entities lived in isolation from each other, much less in isolation from the person living them. They are ways of speaking about a relationship with Jesus, words we use to speak what cannot be adequately spoken, ways to "eff" the ineffable. A religious is called to a particular way (admitting of myriad diverse forms) of being a Christian, of being, therefore, a loving presence of Jesus in the world. Each individual does that in his own way, but within a religious community in a commonality of purpose with other like-minded women or men. The point is, I cannot be chaste and not poor, in relationship to Jesus; I cannot be obedient but not chaste or chaste but not obedient. I am one person, a whole, a unity. My relationship with the Lord is unified. We apply terms like "poor," "chaste," "obedient," but we know we are speaking about a particular person, me, in relationship to another person, Jesus, and just taking part of that single relationship at a time.

I suggest that we have always talked about religious life as a vocation, and it may be helpful to speak of its parts as vocations also. The day I was ordained a priest I was not yet a priest, but was, in faith, called to become one. Likewise, the day I took first vows, or even the day I pronounced final vows, I was not yet a religious, was not yet poor, chaste, obedient, but I was formally accepting God's call to me to become more so.

Much of what I have to say as I look at religious life in these pages simply builds upon this basic, and perhaps incredibly apparent (but, I think, neglected, forgotten, even, at least in practice, denied) verity. A religious is not a poor person, but is one called in a particular way, within a community, with a particular charism, to become more and more a sign of dependence upon the Lord, more and more a receiver of everything, owner of nothing, sharer of all, in a love relationship with an incredible Jesus. Neither I, nor anyone else, was a celibate lover, a chaste person the day I took vows. A lifelong project may help me to become more so, more aware of God's love for me, more open to sharing that love everywhere, with everyone, more free, less afraid, more open, less needy, but celibacy is a prayerfully learned art, not a once-and-for-all given.

And, if obedience is, as it must be, a lifelong response to the God of history, leading us through time and circumstances constantly changing, certainly no one ever *is* obedient, but he may be always becoming so.

We have often in the past spoken of religious vows in a negative, denying way. I can perhaps say a definitive "no." I can promise never to own anything, never to sleep with anyone, never to make personal isolated decisions, and do that once and for all. But if the vows are positive statements about a living, growing, changing, dynamic relationship with the Lord, then they speak of gradual, vocational growth into progressively more and more freedom. A person can keep vows negatively and be dead. To be alive in the Lord means to accept a challenge, a call, a promise, and to try to grow into it.

The chapters that follow suggest some elements of growth, change, progression in this vocation that we call religious life. It may help if I first indicate what I consider religious life to be a call to, a project of, today.

The Project and the Risk

I have been deeply influenced by my own tradition. The language of Ignatius and its contemporary phrasing in the Society of Jesus frame the words I use to speak my own vision of religious life. As I worked with sisters from a variety of communities in Lesotho, a very different country and culture, I found myself beginning with a description of religious life based on my own community's Thirty-second Congregation, specifically the document on "Jesuits Today." Through dialogue and discussion a brief description of religious life emerged on which we all agreed. I present it here as a descriptive starting point for the parts that follow. The description is not complete, nor does it totally distinguish the religious from other ways of being Christian, but it provides the opportunity for you to see if I am talking about the same thing that you are trying to live. After the definition I suggest the challenge and the risk such a project entails.

Descriptive Definition:

A religious is a person, a Christian sinner, called and loved by God, for a mission of service to all. A religious responds freely and totally by witnessing within an ecclesial community and communion that is constantly being formed by the gospel

7

and centered in the Eucharist, that is, in Christ, in order to co-create a world that is at once more human and more divine. Let us look at the parts of this description.

A religious is a person: We come to religious life, or any life, with all that it means to be a person, a unique, mysterious combination of flesh and spirit, neither angel, nor animal, and certainly not ourselves divine. We begin with all the glories and the grubbies of our personhood.

A Christian sinner, called and loved by God: The beginning of adult life, and therefore of Christian life, seems that basic realization that I am at one and the same time a sinner, and a called, loved, chosen, redeemed sinner. The realization of a deep and lasting need for a redeemer and the joy that the redeemer is at hand underlie any life stance within the Christian community. The religious is not unlike other Christians, set apart, sinless, but one of them, called to the same universal holiness, in the same dependency on the Lord. We embrace religious life not so much because we think it is a good idea, or because it is better than some other form of life, but because in some mysterious way, we are invited to such a life by the Lord.

Responded to freely and totally: We try to capture this response by the traditional language and categories of the vows which speak of a kind of totality and depend for their meaning on the freedom with which they are spoken. Authentic religion in any mode of life demands a deep and growing freedom. One does not have to be a religious by any external "ought," but that person moves there through a growing internal conviction of its rightness for himself. This "rightness" however dimly seen moves one to some permanent, wholehearted movement of life, with all the totality that fragmented human beings can possess. Unless the commitment of a religious to this form of life and service is, at once, both free and total (given all the limitations of those words when applied to human acts) we are speaking of a different project than what I would term "religious life."

Witnessing within an ecclesial community and communion:

Religious life never exists meaningfully without clear and subordinate relationship to that larger community, the Church. We exist within that greater Body of Christ and understand our role in relationship to the larger call to all the Church's people to one holiness and a unity in Christ. But, given this relationship, religious accept a call to witness to a particular way of living and loving within the larger community, as separate and supportive sub-community with particular relationships and mission that are its own. This community within the Church is more than just a gathering of friends, or like-minded people, for it is, or ought to be, moving towards true communion, the union of minds and hearts in shared life and service.

This communion is constantly being formed by the gospel and centered in the Eucharist: Religious life in which Jesus is not the living center, the motivating force, the envisioned end, becomes a hoax, a sham, destructive of the individuals within the group and any apparent service the community may perform. Only the community that constantly turns back to the pages and the person of the New Testament, seeing how this lived Word speaks to them today, only the community that draws its strength from the table of the Lord, recognizing their leader in the breaking of the bread, only the community that is on its way to becoming more and more the incarnation of Jesus, is a religious community. This is something we admittedly move towards rather than arrive at, but when the centrality is lost, the project changed, we have become something other than we began to be. If our life centers around a particular apostolic work, or a rule book, or even papal decrees, rather than the person of Jesus, we have ceased, in the deepest sense, to be religious.

In all of the above, there is a single purpose, *to co-create a world that is at once more human and more divine*: There are not two worlds, one graced and the other graceless, one supernatural, the other natural. There is only one world, this world, our world, God's world. We do not so much ask God to create his kingdom among us as experience him inviting us to let him live and work in us to create this kingdom. As Christians, we believe in Jesus, and in him the divine and human become one. A world of justice, love, and peace as Jesus envisaged it would be both perfectly human (as he was) and perfectly mirror the divine (which he did). The religious today is not one who escapes from the world, but rather is immersed in it, committed to it, challenged by it, hoping for it. The Our Father is not so much a prayer we pray as a commitment we make. We pledge ourselves to try to establish the Lord of heaven, as also the Lord of this world where his kingdom is coming. We promise to struggle until the order of this world more closely mirrors the order of the heavens, where all receive enough to eat each day and where the forgiveness between us reflects the forgiveness we want the Lord to have toward us. In other words, prayer and life, religious life and secular life, human and divine, are all a single unit.

This abstract and lofty description is perhaps the star we shoot at if we are ever to hit a thistle top, but I offer it to frame our discussion of religious life and its project today. We are not some kind of other-worldly, distant, separate group, but bodies of people within the people of God, within the world, helping the Church to be Church. We are not so much concerned with the salvation of our own souls (Jesus already assures us of that and we are called to spread the Good News). We are not people proud that we have been called but humbled that we can serve.

Admittedly I have not done very much to identify the religious in a way that distinguishes him from other committed Christians. Perhaps we do not need to as the false distinctions were too clear for too long. There is, of course, a communal dimension to religious life, but many Christians today are parts of sub-communities of various kinds. We do speak vows, but every Christian is called to be poor, chaste, obedient. Both the centering of life in Christ and the mission of service to the world are common to any baptized, responsive person. Whatever distinguishing mark there may be seems to lie somehow in nuance, angle, composite, rather than in any clearly defined concept. Let me reflect on that for a moment. I suggest that religious life, consciously and freely undertaken, is distinguished from the life of other Christians only in that it maximizes the risk common to all Christians, the risk of faith. The religious commits himself to living out the gospel in radical form. This form differs from the common and challenging enough dimension shared with others. Religious vows, more in what they entail than in their wording, put a person into a stark situation of relying on the power of God, taking a risk by not utilizing the ordinary means of growth common to, and challenging of, most people. Each vow specifies a dimension of that risk.

Most people grow to be responsible by constantly having to come to grips with the goods of the earth. The religious who misunderstands or abuses the vow of poverty, who is satisfied with mere (and often childish) dependence, runs a risk of never becoming responsible. To step outside the ordinary manner of becoming responsible for the goods of the earth, the care of oneself and others, demands a kind of radical dependence on the Lord who will provide. Too easily a religious becomes a materially secure, communally cared for, irresponsible person, an unchristian person. The risk is very real.

Most people grow in the deepest Christian virtue, the ability to love and to accept love, by entering into a particular committed, challenging love relationship with another human being, husband or wife, and the eventual similar demands of loving parenthood. The religious who risks a loving, single life steps outside this ordinary mode, trusting that the Lord will lead him to love, and to accept love in other, more mysterious ways. But it is too easy for a religious to avoid loving anyone because he does not have to love specific someones. Again, the risk is real.

Most people learn to be mature by having to make their own decisions, determine the direction of their own lives, discern where the Lord and their own history lead them. The religious steps outside this ordinary mode and commits himself to seeing life within a communal context. And that person can, again, too easily relinquish all decision-making power into the hands of another. We risk remaining terribly immature. Through the composite relationship with the Lord that the vows address, the religious risks immaturity, irresponsibility, unloving, meaningless life. The vows do not have to lead to such an end, but they can, and admittedly, too often do. There is a sense in which the religious must realize that there is very little "middle" possible to him between becoming a saint or a "slob," of either really walking on those waters or sinking and drowning totally.

We cannot picture our lives as the surrendering of very bad things . . . material goods, sexual love, our own will. These are good things. All created things are good, but perhaps not good enough, and so we choose to witness to a life of faith, relying on God more than on the riches and beauties of the world. The vows do speak of renunciation, but not of something undesirable. They are the renunciation of a high good, but not the values represented by them; a renunciation *for* not *from* . . . for something, someone greater. We must love the world passionately if we are to passionately love Jesus more.

In all of the above I express a fuzzy understanding of what I am already trying to live. I do not apologize for this. I say it this way to encourage myself, and all of us to re-think, and hopefully revive the dynamism of our lives, to question what we are doing, and how we are doing it. The succeeding chapters suggest some lines of thought regarding each vow to sharpen our focus and deepen our lives.

· 3 ·

Poverty: Open-handed Love and Open-hearted Sharing

My understanding of the project of religious poverty flows haltingly from an effort to understand my own experience. I have for years been strangely frightened by the vow, at least by the inadequate word we use to express it. Jesuits habitually take final vows, sometime after ordination to the priesthood, although we make a perpetual profession in the end of novitiate. I had been ordained, had even been a superior for some years and found myself postponing that final, public statement, and not knowing fully why. It had something to do with my own feelings of inadequacy, something to do with an idealistic hope that the Jesuits would become perfect, in which case I could, with perfect confidence, join definitively a parousiac community. For the most part, however, it had to do with the wording of the vows and the struggle to understand them in a way that made it seem honest to voice my continued commitment. This centered chiefly on the vow of poverty.

It seemed one thing to commit myself to the Jesuits at age twenty and to use the traditional, partially understood language. I was honestly trying to live out my commitment to the Society, Church, people. But I could not wholeheartedly stand up in front of people and say that I vowed poverty with the same ease some fifteen or eighteen years later. I lived in a very comfortable home, with more than plenty to eat and drink. I had an automobile at my disposal. I had more security towards the material aspect of my future than the vast majority of human beings. I had access to medical and dental care of the finest kind, and an education that few in America, not to mention the rest of the world, enjoy. Whatever else I was, I was not, nor did I seem to be trying to be, poor.

I wrestled with all the post-Vatican II language about simplicity of life, identification with the poor, the quest for justice, and I found these notions both challenging and gospel-accurate. But I was and am not sure that poverty is a value rather than a negative fact, as understood by most of our age. My problem was, on one level, a language problem, but it was also a difficulty that had to do with understanding what the project might be that the word "poverty" was supposed to delineate.

I finally made my final profession as a Jesuit, in the midst of this confusion, without the clarity I sought for because it seemed sufficiently important to my Jesuit friends to say, in whatever language, that I would be with them. Final incorporation into the Society of Jesus became more important than the language such incorporation was couched in. But the confusion remained.

The year I spent working with religious communities in Lesotho, in Southern Africa, clarified the question. The language of "poverty" became even less satisfying, but an approach to at least a personal answer began to emerge. In Lesotho the Church is only one-hundred years old. Missionaries, largely French-Canadian, had done an excellent job of spreading Christian doctrine throughout the country. Religious communities were flourishing, and the vast majority in every community were now native Basotho people when I arrived in the summer of 1977.

The people of Lesotho are very poor; the average per-capita income is somewhere around $104. People sleep in huts, live off the land, struggle to survive. But the religious have adopted largely western ways, influenced by the missionaries. They sleep in houses, eat solid, well-prepared food, avoid the insecurities of weather, are generally better educated, better housed, better fed. When a native woman joins a religious community, although she gives up much in terms of family and culture, she does move far up the economic scale. The Church, and religious communities within the Church, are seen by the natives as very, very wealthy, powerful, providing them in their villages with health, education, and other services, but rather from above than across a common bond of shared faith. The situation is historically understandable but presently lamentable. If it is true that I, in America, as a religious am not poor, the situation in Lesotho is the same in capital letters, underlined in red.

If an American sister lives in a neighborhood in a poor house, she usually very quickly makes the house lovely, warm, artistic. If a Basotho sister moved into a hut in the village, she would quickly decorate, modernize, improve the hut. In either case their education and their security would be far more than that of the surrounding population. The effort to become poor, to live more simply, is quite admirable and becomes increasingly important in the Church, in any country, but the one making the effort will never really be seen as poor. The project to become more poor, to have less, even to use less, though it possesses some good and important elements, is not the right project for what we profess by our poorly worded vow. We are, and will continue to be, rich in grace, in personal qualities, in opportunities, and in material goods. The only hope we have for meaningful witness, it seems to me, is to admit this, and to admit also that what we have is not ours, but must be shared. I want to develop this point, so let me back up just a bit.

I have lived with many men who were totally admirable in their effort to live poorly. They rarely bought clothes, drove always the worst car, used public transportation or their feet whenever possible. They did not go outside their community for food or recreation, and they used what the community provided sparingly. They were models of a type of poverty.

But they still appeared rich. The home they lived in was nice, often huge for it housed fifty or sixty people. The material goods were there, whether or not they used them. They were not poor because they had to be, and hence were not seen as poor, however much they were seen as holy, men. In Lesotho, likewise, I saw many sisters and priests living individually poor lives, simple lives. They asked permission for everything, had small or non-existent personal budgets, were models of a style of poverty inherited from the missionaries. But they still appeared rich, as the Church appeared rich. They still lived in a nice house, slept in a warm bed, were provided with good food, even if they chose to eat it in a single dish. They looked wealthy because they were part of something that so appeared. No matter how hard the priests I have known, or the sisters I saw in Lesotho, or any other religious tries, they will still have great trouble witnessing as parts of a contemporary community to anything by this "poorer and poorer" understanding of our vow of poverty. Any single individual as part of a group, by very reason of that group, will fail in their project if this mentality continues to be, in fact, *the* project.

There are many things that can and ought to be said about poverty, but I want to make one simple point. If the vow is to mean anything today (among other things connected with it: thirst for justice, commitment to the needs of the most poor, challenge to existing systems that continue the inequities of our age), it will have to do much *more with sharing than with not having.* The vow of poverty should be renamed and called a vow to (open-hearted love and open-handed) sharing. We possess so much, not just in things. It is not ours, but gift. We hold it all in stewardship, and must share it broadly, deeply, freely, generously, whatever the *it* might be.

If there is a scandal in religious life today, it is not that religious have so much, but that they protect it so tightly, and share it so grudgingly. We see so many religious houses where others than their community are not welcomed in the dining room, much less in the house, where time and talent and goods are seen as possessions, not gifts to be shared. Often in Lesotho the missions were rimmed with tall, barbwire fences, proclaiming loudly that all that was within belonged, not to the people, but to the priests and sisters there. What do the locked and fenced doors of our houses say except that we are protecting something we do not really own. The same is true of the locked doors of our hearts.

The best way I can draw this to a head is to describe the "poor" or sharing community as I would envision it. The religious house must be a place where greatly gifted people, aware that all they have and are is gift, share freely of those gifts with any and with all. The community of sisters living together is a witnessing part of the community where they live. Their time, their food, their very communal life, especially of prayer, should benefit everyone. People share their meals, come to their liturgies, pray quietly with them in their chapel. Their rooms are places for people to talk with them of God or of their own struggles to be more human. They need perhaps to reserve some time, some space, to be a community themselves, but this is small in every way but quality; otherwise they are there for others.

Personally, I have received a superior education. It is not mine, but to be shared, and I want to continue to read, pray, think, and share the fruit of that with anyone who wants it. I eat well and want to share my meals with people I work with, care about, or anyone who needs to share my food. It is not mine. I am lucky, usually, to live with prayerful men. I want to share that prayer, that faith, with those around me, to nourish and strengthen them in faith. I would like all the locks of my life, on doors or hearts, to be changed to "Welcome" signs, inviting people to benefit from any way that God has gifted me or us.

All around me I have heard people, dealing with the subject of poverty as sharing, insist on the need for privacy. I grant that need to some degree, but I suggest that my vow of poverty is a vow to minimize that need because I am free to gift others with what is not mine.

The most serious failure in poverty on the part of most religious has nothing to do with things, but it is the refusal to share themselves, their prayer life, their faith and hope, their love with their brothers and sisters, both in community and out. The refusal to speak at a community meeting is rarely seen as hoarding, possessiveness, but it most surely is. The lack of concern about a sister next door is a failure to get outside myself, and share my time, my heart, or even my feeling of poverty ("I don't know what to do . . . or say") with another. The only sense I can make of the words we glibly say is that deepest gospel value of knowing we/I have been loved and blessed, and we cannot help but share.

Clearly this approach to the vow of poverty cannot be lived in isolation, but must become the project of a group, deciding to open up its entire lifestyle as a community to witness to our common giftedness. Perhaps more than the other two vows, poverty is not, cannot be a private vow, but one taken within community. Together we need to see how gifted we all are, and we call each other to ever more generous sharing.

So many religious today experience deeply the frustration of knowing they are not poor, yet they live in communities that will not unlock their doors, open their dining rooms, free their chapels, and most importantly share their lives with the people around them. There is, it seems, nothing more deadening to the spirit than to make a vow that I am institutionally incapable of fulfilling, by reason of that very institution within which I took the vow. Yet that is the situation for many of us today.

I suggest, moreover, that the role of superior within a religious community is quite central to the living of this vow. Superiors need not give permission to others to buy, sell, use, or share the common goods. Adults can make those decisions themselves. But the superior can be the one who calls the community to reflect on its giftedness, who discerns with them how best and prudently these gifts can be shared within the community and without. How can those needy around them be fed, whether that food is meat indeed, or prayer, or time, or energies, education, insight, suffering? We need to be called to this sharing more and more as groups of committed Christians so we can witness together as Christians that in having Jesus we need nothing else.

A community of religious people, banded together for common witness and common service, tries to proclaim that they are rich because Christ is theirs. In this richness they can afford to be poor. They proclaim together that being is more important than having, that people are more important than things, that whatever they may appear to have is not theirs but God's and, therefore, everyone's.

Finally, in a world where many, many people are in fact poor, hungry, oppressed, we do not need communities that try to be artificially poor, but those, that being rich, can share. That refers to every community from a nation to the small group of sisters living in a neighborhood. We need to live more simply because we are sharing more. We need to be more concerned with justice because we share in the sufferings of people scarred by injustices. We need to share more deeply in the lives of those who are truly poor because we share in the awareness that we too possess nothing, however much we may hold in trust. Any other project today is not worthy of our energies, and it does not capture what is behind the vow we make and must try to live.

. *4* .

Becoming a Celibate Lover

We never know how we are doing at something unless we are quite sure what it is we are trying to do. That seems obvious, but for a long time in religious life we have not been very clear on what it is we aim at, what our project, outlined by the vows, proposed. Thus our evaluation of progress individually and corporately has been similarly muddled.

So often the project of poverty appeared to be to become poorer and poorer, have less and less, flee from any use of, much less dependency on material things. The previous chapter speaks of simplicity of life, and rightly so, but our education, tastes, mobility, and security, leave us looking, if not being, richer than most around us. If we redirect our aim to the Lukan concept of stewardship and see ourselves as keepers, rather than owners, and our vow as one that commits us to sharing life and service, our project changes. It becomes possible and, in fact, more Christian. Poverty that aims at sharing everything, rather than possessing nothing, or little, becomes a gospel virtue and not just a discouraging task.

Something akin to this happens in the vow of chastity or celibacy. Consciously or not, many religious seem to be trying harder and harder to love God more and more, seem to strive to be less and less involved with, responsible towards human beings. We seem in fact, sometimes, to hold an angelic rather than human ideal. With no yardstick to measure our progress, we create a false one or give in to discouragement at the inability to achieve this angelic state.

I want to suggest a way of looking at the project of celibacy, or, more precisely, the project of becoming what I would call a celibate lover, for that is what we are called to be: not just lovers, and not just celibate, but both. There is no virtue in simply being celibate, unmarried, unsexed as it were. There is deep virtue in loving, or even trying to love, as God loves us: freely, deeply, broadly, unpossessively.

When we look at our religious project, we need honestly to admit that failures can come from two directions, not just one. We can be, in a sense, too loving, or too celibate (though obviously "too loving" is a contradiction in terms). We can be too careful, too distant, too cold . . . too celibate. Or we can love unwisely, insensitively, possessively, manipulatively . . . too (falsely) loving. But we can fail on either side. The religious who has three pampered dogs and no friends fails to live his vow as much as the religious with a mistress for both fail to live out the call they professed to answer. We can, then, fail in either of two directions. Just as importantly, we will fail! Only Jesus did not.

If we see our lives as aiming at becoming more and more loving, more and more celibate, and hope to become an integrated combination of both by the time of death, we see, schematically, our project. Every human being will wander from that line, being at times either too careful or too free, too intimate or too distant, too involved or too uncaring. We can manipulate the feelings of people, dominating their emotions to our own selfish or needy ends. We can also manipulate the minds of people in a feelingless insensitivity to the freedom that is theirs to be. Both are failures.

Please note: I am not talking about loving only God in a celibate way. I am talking about loving real skin and bones, body and soul, flesh and spirit, human people. The kind Jesus asks us to love. This needs some clarification.

Many religious seem to think that they are called to love God alone, despite what the gospels always and everywhere say. A vow to love God exclusively would be unchristian, in-human, and impossible. Jesus tells us, "This is my command-ment, that you love one another as I have loved you" (Jn. 15:12). St. John writes, "Beloved, if God so loved us, we also ought to love one another" (1 Jn. 4:11). In fact, we search the New Testament in vain to find somewhere where we are asked to love God directly. Jesus and his followers continually indi-cate that the movement of grace is from God to us, and from us to others (not back to God).

How many try to live out their vow of celibacy by spending more and more time in prayer (not a bad thing in itself, if right-headed) trying to show God how much they love him and that they are totally his. But a Christian actually goes (or should go) to prayer *to let God love him or her.*

Read that last phrase over again; it is an important and neglected concept. We go to prayer to deepen our sense and conviction that God loves us, from which we can move, in his Spirit, towards a world that needs to experience that love incarnated in people like ourselves. Nothing in Scripture says that we show God our love for him by how often or how deeply we pray, how frequently we participate at Mass, the vigils we keep. All kinds of things indicate that we are sent to show his love for others, having first received it ourselves. So we go to prayer to know God's love for us, and we must go there honestly, deeply, often. But whether or not that prayer has been fruitful is not measured by how good it feels at the time, or by the great insights we derived, unless that feeling, that insight leads us to be a more loving presence of Jesus towards his people.

So, the project of our vow of celibacy is not just to love God and not just to stay celibate, i.e. unmarried, without inter-course. The project is to love and yet remain honest, free, mobile, able to carry the Lord's love where it is needed next and most.

Perhaps we need to be convinced that celibacy is a vow to love. Well, it is a vow of Christian women and men, after all, and Christianity itself is a baptismally based vow to love, whether celibate or not. It is, I am presuming, more important to be Christian than to be celibate. Celibacy must be a vow to love, a way, a style of loving, of witnessing to God's love.

Every Christian continues the mission of Christ, to bring liberty to captives, sight to the blind, hearing to the deaf, good news to the poor (Lk. 4:18 ff.). Every Christian is invited to love one's enemies, to do good to those who hate them (Lk. 6:27), and to take seriously the injunction: "Be merciful, even as your Father is merciful" (Lk. 6:36). We are all called to be ready to forgive and hence to be vulnerable to the failures of others, not just once or twice, or seven times, but seventy times seven times (Mt. 18:21–22).

In Matthew's twenty-fifth chapter the entire basis on which our life will be evaluated is in terms of love: did you feed, visit, clothe, love me? We know that but somehow we fail to connect it with our life of the vows. At the end of our lives, Jesus, our judge, will not (if Matthew is correct) ask whether we had sexual relations with anyone, or how many hours we prayed, or how many vows we took (though, hopefully, our answers to these questions will help us to answer positively the really important question). He will ask us whether we loved anyone.

So the vows we take, and celibacy in particular, are as valid as they free us to love, broadly, deeply, honestly those the Lord sends us.

Now it would be easier if it were true that we can love in general, but it is not, and we cannot. We could, perhaps, say with Lucy in the Peanuts cartoon: "I love mankind, it's people I can't stand." But to love really means to choose to care about individual people, men and women, good and bad, nice and not so nice. It means being vulnerable to them, able to hurt them, and be hurt by them, and, more importantly, to call them to life. It means, not being afraid, "Perfect love casts out fear" (1 Jn. 4:18). It does not mean that our perfect love takes away our fear, but that God's love for us makes us less and less afraid to love concrete, specific human beings. Jesus in the gospels is portrayed as saving all people, but specifically by loving John and Martha, Mary and Lazarus, and Zaccheus, and me and you. He was able to change lives because he cared about people. To do so he was able to be deeply hurt by them, "Could you not watch with me one hour?" (Mt. 26:40), or "Judas, would you betray the Son of Man with a kiss?" (Lk. 22:48).

As I write these lines I do believe deeply in what I say, but I do not want to appear to be naive. I realize that the religious who try to live this out, to love as God loves them, will encounter problems. They will need to become extremely prayerful (i.e. aware of God's deep personal love for them) if they are to truly love human beings and not try to hold on, to control, to possess, or be possessed by them. The longings of their human, sexual natures will arise, confusing good and healthy relationships. This will happen when least wanted, least expected. Because they are not Jesus, they will fail, as they try to learn to be celibate lovers. But these failures can at least be Christian failures, in the right direction, a falling forward rather than a falling back, and we can learn from them and go on.

Too often the Church, or a community within the Church, has judged and punished those human frailties occurring in the person honestly trying to learn to love, and it has not even noticed those failures of distance, coldness, and aloofness that destroy the Church and Christ's call to union so that the world can believe. We decide to expel the very apostolic young man admitting to homosexual tendencies, generally under control, and ordain men with no close friends, who, in fact, fear intimacy.

In every generation of religious life there have been too many crusty bachelors and mean old maids masquerading as celibates, going to their graves without once letting sex rear its head. Too often love was squelched in the process, and they witnessed to nothing but will power. What the world needs, the witness we are called to place alongside the sacramental witness of committed married love, is that there is a human possibility of loving and not having to possess or be possessed, a human possibility of loving and not holding on or being held on to. We are called to witness to a love that is one facet of the love of God for his people, a love that moves over rich and poor alike, over the beautiful people and the not so beautiful, over the alive and the not so alive.

I do not want to minimize the risk involved in living such a project. We risk involvement and pain, risk even sin and separation from our community or priesthood, risk, in myriad ways, the cross. But I would emphasize that the risk involved in any other project is perhaps more grave. For it is the risk to fail to be a Christian, to fail to love at all. As John Courtney Murray pointed out many years ago, in choosing not to love anyone particularly, personally, uniquely, we risk never loving at all, never being alive at all, never letting Jesus be alive in us.

Let me emphasize a point already made. No one can fulfill in any successful way the project of becoming a celibate lover without a deep, enduring life of prayer. No one can reach out in an effort to really care for other human beings unless they know day in and day out how cared for they are themselves. It is only since God first loved us that we can try to love one another in his fashion. We cannot become celibate lovers if we are trying to make up for the absence of this love of God for us by the multiplicity or depth of our relationships with others. We cannot give what we do not have.

Finally, celibacy is a vow that only becomes Christian, only ultimately is possible within a community. A religious promises to support others in their project, and to accept, even to demand support for himself or herself. How often it is sadly the case that a religious struggling to love and yet be integrated within an overall commitment finds himself or herself isolated from or judged by the community. How often we fail to reach out a hand to someone hurting, believing it to be none of our business? How frequently has every community talked at meetings of other things?

We talk, for example, endlessly about poverty: simplicity of life, personal budget, personal or communal lifestyle concerning clothes, travel, or recreation. And we easily and often discuss and debate the obedience involved in a discernment process, in corporate versus personal apostolate, our mission from Church and community. And these are good things to discuss. But how rarely we talk about our corporate struggle to become celibate lovers. This struggle rarely surfaces except between intimate friends. Generally we bury our fears or temptations, failures and successes, and struggle on alone. Too often we seem to be the only one struggling while the dimming vision seems unique. We search out a director to do what our next door neighbor could better accomplish if only she were not afraid, or he were more sensitive, if only they would listen, care, share their own bent or broken dreams. In fact, it seems to me that the possibility of living out a loving celibacy is in direct proportion to a community's ability to talk openly about the subject. How few communities provide such support!

My point in all of this is simply to insist that the vow of celibacy is a part of the overall communal commitment and communal project. Our convents, rectories, religious houses must be homes where brothers and sisters challenge each other to laughter and to love, where failures are accepted and hope is nourished. The witness we give is given together, founded on the great love God has, not just for me, but for us, from which we turn together from a deeply shared life to a work of service together.

I began by saying that we can never know how we are doing unless we are clear on what it is we are trying to do. I suggest that this chapter indicates a neglected part of that project. If we agreed and helped each other along the path, all of us who seriously try to be religious men or women could better distinguish than we have been able to do in a long time how we are progressing.

. 5 .

Obedience: The Vow to Pray

Every aspect of life, religious, Christian, human life reminds us how much easier it is to say no than yes. A no can be definitive, final, once-and-for-all. A yes must be repeated, deepened, constantly new, or else it becomes, ultimately, a no, whatever our lips may be saying. Because the vow of obedience is radically a saying yes to the lead of God's Spirit in our lives, it is a yes that must be constantly affirmed, renewed as circumstances change, deepened as our knowledge of our self, our world, our God is deepened.

Many of us, trained in a *via negativa*, perhaps originally saw the vow of obedience in a negative fashion. We said that we would no longer do our own will, no longer question, no longer be selfish, but would let superiors and community dispose of us as they saw fit. We said no to self will forever. Perhaps it seemed final, definite at the time. As we live it out it becomes constantly apparent that a series of yeses had to flesh out that no. And if virtue has been internalized at all, we come to realize that each new assignment, or nuance of an assignment, has to become our own, our choice, not just accepted but embraced, if our presence in whatever task we undertake is to be a Christian, loving, giving, totally present, presence.

I would like to expose, from a thousand things that could be spoken of relative to obedience, only a particular, perhaps neglected, aspect of this vow: *the complexity of the promise*, in its process-like character, its intimate connection with our life of prayer, and our own personal responsibility.

Because it is a yes, rather than a no, the vow of obedience is a complex promise to fulfill. As an assent to the leading of the Lord of history, the Lord of our lives, it includes many elements, constantly held in tandem, constantly only partially comprehended, always somewhat inadequately realized. I will consider the role of the superior or leader of the community elsewhere, but here I will consider what it means for a religious to try to be faithful to the promise he or she has made. I will speak here only of the movement towards this or that apostolic mission—what has been called in the past our "status," or "obedience," our apostolic assignment.

I am presuming, perhaps gratuitously, that the experiences in our age like the Holocaust and Watergate have put to rest the belief that there can be virtue in simply doing what one is told because of the authority of the one telling. Blind, unreflective assent to commands is neither Christian nor human. Vatican II and everything since indicate the gift of the Spirit to each individual, a gift which is also a burden for it implies a responsibility towards and a response to that Spirit moving within one's heart as well as the community and the external world as a whole. The living out of a promise of obedience implies a being in touch with oneself, one's community, one's world.

We remind ourselves, too, that our obedience is not ultimately to our religious community, nor even to the Church as such, but an obedience to God, whose Spirit leads us, within Church and community. The obedience of Jesus, an obedience which led to cross and resurrection, impelled him to often be misunderstood by his family (his community), to be at odds with religious understandings commonly held, to break traditions and even laws when the love of persons demanded. It was more critical for him to be a good, honest, authentic human being than to be what was considered a good Jew, and so he spoke with women on and of the street, with tax collectors, broke the Sabbath laws upon occasion, let God's Spirit lead him. It is more important for me to be myself as God leads me, to be an authentic, honest, human being than to be a Jesuit or a priest. Hopefully the conflicts and contradictions are rare or nonexistent, but this principle indicates the complexity of following a vow that is not a simple submission to existing structures or systems of authority that relate to me. Our obedience is to be like the obedience of Jesus, not the obedience of John Mitchell (obediently following his president) or Adolph Eichmann (obediently exterminating six million Jewish people).

Let me spell out in somewhat simple form what seem the necessary steps of an individual religious today in trying to be faithful to a promise made. We have promised obedience within a particular community in order to serve the Church and the world. We have said that we would no longer make our decisions in a solitary, isolated fashion, but in the light of the group with which we have bound ourselves by vows, the Church of which that community is a part, and the world to which that Church is committed. Each of these realities gives a nuance to our vow.

A religious commits himself or herself to openness to the community. I promise to be totally, vulnerably honest with my superiors. If they are to help me to be used within the community for service to the Church, they must know me as I am, might be, wish to be. That means I tell them, as best I can, my gifts, talents, calls, fears, temptations, failures. I tell them my vision of the world, my own assessment of myself.

One often hears another religious say, or feels deeply oneself, that if my superior knows me, he will judge me harshly, criticize me, even expel me. That risk must continually be taken. If a community does not want me as I am then, I am not called by God to that community. If they do not want me, warts and all, they do not want me, but some pretended image of me. Obedience means warts and all. Many religious have been badly misplaced, even dehumanized, by the way obedience has functioned in their lives often because they did not sufficiently reveal who they really were to their community, and, though superiors were blamed, the fault lay, frequently, in the lack of openness by the individual. To let God lead us by our promise within a community, we vow, first of all, to be as honestly open with that community, superiors and others, as we possibly can.

To be open and honest with others presupposes that I am open and honest with myself. I cannot tell you about me, unless I know me. I have often, in retreats, asked people to tell me the best things about themselves, the ways in which God has blessed them, worked through them, gifted them, called them. Many people cannot say. Ask them their faults and weaknesses and they give an almost endless, certainly comprehensive list. To be obedient to the Spirit of God calling me, means to see the beauty of the me he is calling.

I love the poster which pictures a junkyard of empty beer cans, rotting boxes, odds and ends of garbage, with the caption over it, "God don't make junk!" God does not make junk, nor did he make a mistake when he turned out the particular model that is me. As Ephesians points out, I am God's work of art. I need to know the beauty of that work, of myself, if I am to see how God can use me in his kingdom. I need to know how deeply loved I am by God, the ways in which he has held me in the palm of his hand, has called me by name. And I need to be able honestly to share that giftedness with others, with my community. This is deeply connected with the living out of the vow of obedience, to grow continually in the knowledge of myself, and in particular my giftedness, in order to put that gift at the disposal of the community—religious, Church, world.

Certainly I must also know my faults, failings, fears, and share these too. In fact, I need to share not just my faults, but the root causes of them if I can grasp them. I need to be open about myself as sinner, as well as saved. I do not need to pretend to be perfect, however much I need to know that I am good. To be obedient to a living God in a changing world, I need both to know myself as well as I can, a knowledge that will be constantly growing, and to share myself as best I can with my community, particularly my superiors.

Third, to be obedient in a way that speaks an even louder yes within a community in the Church, I need to know that community. That knowledge of my community has, at least, two parts, people and vision. I need to know the actual work that people are doing, or preparing to do, their hopes, dreams, fears and foibles, their wonders and their warts. I have committed myself to serving the Church and world within this group, and this implies awareness of individuals that make up this group. If I am to use my talents with them to serve, our mutual knowledge of and sensitivity towards each other must be reciprocal. Our vow is "within community" and the Spirit is given not just to a group but to each individual within that group. The discovery of a community "charism" today as it affects me depends on knowing the "charism" operating in the lives of individuals.

Obviously this has enormous ramifications about style of community life, frequency of community gatherings, the giving of myself to things that promote various forms of getting together. A group of people living good but separate lives cannot be obedient to God's Spirit individually or collectively.

I also need to know the vision, the general "charism," of my community. I need to read, study, pray over the early roots and the recent branches of the community of which I am a part. Acts of chapters, letters from superiors general, position papers of local groups, all are part of my discernment of God's will for me for they help to define the whole of which my life and service are a part. Many religious in recent years have dispensed themselves from trying to capture the spirit in loosely pinned down, more inspirational, or motivational material coming from their congregations. They were more comfortable with an approach that gave specific rules, clear and distinct ideas. But to be obedient today within a community, within the Church, we need to hear the voice of God as spoken today within that group. We need to capture the spirit that blows today.

So, as I try to see where God is leading me both to be and to serve, I listen to my community, individually and corporately, and I see my life within the context of others' lives. I see my service and vision within the context of communal vision and mission. But, further, I need to listen to the voice of that larger community of which I am a part—the local and universal Church.

A religious, serving within the Church, accepts the limitations of that Church, both local and universal, but searches for the voice of God there too. I am part of a diocese. I need to know the directions of the local bishop and/or pastor, and the aspirations of the people of that area as they impinge on me with my gifts, my faults. I do not need to totally assent, but I must hear the priorities that each group sees. If I want to serve, I serve the needs people actually voice, not simply those of my own choosing. And I am part of a larger Church, Roman Catholic, and ecumenical. A religious who is not trying to incorporate into his or her life the call to justice voiced by every recent major papal and episcopal statement does not respond obediently to God. Work for justice is constitutive of the gospel. The consistently voiced call to action on behalf of justice and the effort to pacify the growing split between rich and poor nations and individuals must somehow be part of any truly apostolic action today. Justice is a concrete issue of this moment and probably many moments to come, but it is only one of many. The point is that obedience to God implies in the listening individual an openness to that God as he speaks in the Church, wherever else he may speak.

And God speaks not only in the Church, but in the world, nation, city, neighborhood around us. The hopes, dreams, fears, and struggles here also are part of the ongoing discernment of God's will for the individual religious. No one who does not read the newspapers, watch the news, listen to the voices of our age in media and life, can be obedient to God.

We have neglected that, and, consequently, served where it was convenient or where we had always served before without paying sufficient heed to the vagaries of a rapidly changing world-city.

Every one of the above items add up to the enormously process-like character of obedience as virtue or vow. We are not and cannot be obedient with a single yes or no. We must constantly become more so. Every aspect changes. I change, and I grow in understanding of the person who wears my clothes and thinks my thoughts. I constantly try to reveal that person who is coming to be to a succession of different superiors, within ever-changing communities. The vision of my own community and its personnel keeps shifting, at least slightly, and becoming in their own way. The Church and world are far from static realities. So my response to the Spirit moving within all of this complex is an ever new, ever more alive response, or it becomes no response at all. Mobility and adaptability must characterize the promise we make to respond to God and to try to let him lead our lives.

And so, central to the vow of obedience is the prayer life of the individual religious. In fact, *the promise to be obedient can perhaps best be summarized as a promise to pray*, to listen to the voice of God speaking in all these diverse elements, to synthesize my life around the God of gospel and sacrament. And this kind of prayer is in no way a saying of prayers, a performing of rituals, a putting in time. It is the strange blend of active-passive, thinking-listening interaction with a living God who, I know in faith, wants to speak to me, call me, challenge me, love me. Prayer is not something I do to show God how much I love him, but a deepening paying attention to how much he loves me in the concrete, here-and-now realities of my very specific life. That God who loves me is the One who calls me. We have often stressed, almost to the point of truism, the need of a religious for prayer. Often it has been a kind of ritually authenticating duty, "If you don't pray you cannot be serious about your commitment." Prayer seemed a duty to be performed to prove something to ourselves or to God. The connection seems to me to be starkly and unmistakably clear. We can only discern where God is leading us if we listen to the divine voice speaking in, through, across, the diverse elements of our life—individual, corporate, ecclesial, cosmic, and microcosmic. Only in prayer can we unite the parts and evolve a holistic response to this divine voice. "I vow obedience" means "I promise to pray," with everything that simple word can mean. Like Jesus, who had to withdraw to desert, mountain, garden, we must withdraw to understand, feel, put together in ever new forms the particulars of our response.

This leads me to my final point. A religious must be responsible for his own decisions. If I teach in a school, do parish visiting, run a hospital, do community organizing, or any of the many apostolic roles available to me today, that service must ultimately be my choice, my responsibility, my yes. It cannot be something forced on me from above without my assent. There must be dialogue with my community, my superiors; there must be openness to the directions they indicate. There cannot be passive, "dead-man's staff" submission to anything that is not clearly (or as clearly as humans are capable of) seen as God's call, God's will for me.

I do not minimize the role of a superior in assigning people. It is important, and in a very deep sense it is the bottom line, the final word. But before that final word must come the deep yes of the individual, a yes that fits the religious as found at this time, in this community, in this Church, in this world. The individual, working in dialogue with all these elements must live that yes, and so it must be his or her personal yes.

The superior speaks the final word to *mission* the individual as part of this community to the mode of service to which that yes specifies commitment. We are sent by our community, but as God sends us, not according to the whim or partially informed opinion of a superior.

At least a major part of any religious' commitment to the Lord within this given group is the hope to really be of service to the community of people needing God's love. Obedience has long been seen as the vow that specifies that service. While agreeing with that traditional understanding, I would add that obedience indicates the elements, the subject matter, and the results of the prayer that can render that service messianic, salvific, a response to God's will. Anything less than such prayerful obedience is unworthy of our vow.

. 6 .

Leadership in Religious Communities

In order to balance the discussion about individuals in obedience, I want to say a word on leadership. Mostly, I want to insist that we need it. I grant the unpopularity of the idea. Everyone is against it. Pastors are out; co-pastors are in. Responsibility is shared responsibility. Designated superiors of local communities are replaced by locally elected "coordinators" or abandoned altogether. The very term "superior" sounds anachronistic in an age that recognizes a Spirit given equally to all.

No one wants to return to the day when the school principal also ruled the convent, often with the same style of authority towards adults that put fear into the hearts of third graders. Still, religious communities would well wonder if some specific form of spiritual leadership, by whatever name, might not be demanded still or, perhaps, anew.

I suggest strongly that even local communities of religious need someone officially in charge to call the community to prayer, to be chief discerner in the community's continual search for God's will, to consistently challenge the community to be brothers or sisters to one another, and simply to love each member of the community. This, as I see it, is the task of any leader of community, on whatever level, by whatever name; the task is essential in forming apostolic communities of love.

The first role of one charged with this responsibility, by whatever process chosen, is to call the community to prayer, not just the saying of prayers, but the open voicing of its concerns, needs, hopes, dreams—the searching out of pertinent questions to its life and ministry, the communal search for the leading Spirit of God. This requires the goodwill of each individual, a general spirit of individual prayer in the community, with some priority given to the corporate endeavor by everyone. An individual cannot create this spirit; he or she can only build upon it. But even when this spirit is present it seems to vanish unless one is specifically seen as overall leader, reminding the group of its shared call. So often we have seen the goodwill of a September faith-experience degenerate by April into a barely extended grace-before-meals, when no one is in charge or when the one in charge was simply assigned this task, with no larger responsibility to the group or to the larger religious community.

I have often wished I had a dollar for every sister who belongs to a "superior-less" community whom I have heard crying out for a deeper, richer, more honest sharing of faith-life with her community. Nothing seems to happen; they never get together. The year ends as it began with great goodwill and enormous hopes floundering. Though the causes of such frustration are manifold, I am convinced that the major one lies in the absence of anyone specifically named, with authority to facilitate this central concern of a community's life.

I do not suggest in any way a return to a rigid, inflexible order of the day or even restricted, scheduled "times of prayer." I speak more of a whole style of community life and leadership. One who knows a group of people, is attentive to individual styles, schedules, sensitivities, who listens to these people and truly hears, can find the rhythms that move the group and bring to some shared voicing of those rhythms before God and one another.

The religious community comes together to respond to God's Spirit. The reason for their shared lives and shared faith is not a pious escape from reality or the fulfilling of some abstract duty, but it is the faith-search together for the direction God is leading the group. The leader who calls the group to prayer becomes the listener mainly responsible to hear what the group says in that prayer and to echo it back to them. Though prayer, personal or communal, mainly assures us of God's continued, enduring love for us as individuals and as a people, it also calls us to incarnate that love in our service of his people. Someone within the community must be responsible to see that such incarnation happens.

Concretely, the superior's role becomes more and more to invite a community to deal with issues it faces in a stance of prayer, with decisions arising out of that prayer. Issues of meatless meals, the opening up of a community to visitors, the allocation of funds to needs of justice or charity, house cars and recreation, or any other significant question can be dealt with in prayer. The superior initiates, encourages, oversees, and helps to bring such prayerful dialogue to a Spirit-guided resolution.

In doing this, the community's faith-leader is truly called to challenge the individuals to be brother or sister to each other, to share themselves, to listen to other voices. Disputes continually need mediation, silence needs to be broken, overbearing voices need to be muted. Only a leader, accepted as such by the community, with recognized, if gentle, authority, can succeed in such a task. The community says in effect, "We call you to help us to be our best selves."

Such a called superior, then, tries to love the community, each individual within it. The central Christian task of the one in charge never was, no matter how much it seemed so, to make decisions, assign personnel, correct the stragglers, or oversee finances, but rather, always, to love the community, to help them know that they are loved and to know and love each other.

If communities have become reluctant to have superiors,

individuals have been more reluctant to assume the role. Both reluctances are understandable. A few years of adult living prove that the further up the pole one climbs the more one's rear end shows. No one wants to rise above a group simply to become a better target. There is not and should not be any honor or glamor in the job of leadership within a religious community. It is simply a necessary role of service enabling the outreach service of any community to flourish. It should be assumed only by those who want to serve the community and see value in helping to form that kind of unity for which Jesus prays, "That they may all be one; . . . so that the world may believe that thou hast sent me" (Jn. 17:21). Such a person, assuming such a task, will inevitably face trials.

Perhaps the most critical trial or temptation for the good religious leader lies in the gradual loss of one's own identity. When a sister sympathizes, understands, supports her sisters, each with a different view, need, voice, she can easily lose track of her own convictions. The need to discover constantly in prayer where she is before God becomes acute. And every good leader needs to learn a subtle art or ability to voice one's own conviction, to speak personal beliefs in a way that does not impose itself upon a group, close discussion, hinder the Spirit. The superior's voice within a dialogue is one voice among many, not the final voice, until the community as a whole is able to recognize it as such, because it is not her voice, but theirs.

The above suggests that the good leader of a religious community is rather like the director of a play. The director has a good idea of the play, is familiar with various forms the play has taken in the past, the richness of what is suggested by the author that has never, perhaps, been fully tapped. The director has his or her own idea of the play, a sense of its meaning and method, a view of the possibilities inherent in each part, and yet a sense of mystery and awe towards new possibilities. The director knows that every actor will bring unique gifts, creativity, innovation, and will do his or her part quite personally. His role becomes to harmonize the gifts of all the cast and crew, to integrate, soften or strengthen each part, to get the entire production unified, coherent. He hopes to help balance the two possible extremes: undue individuality or constrictive uniformity. A play will be destroyed if each artist plays his or her part, however well, in disregard for the interpretations and idiosyncrasies of others. It will also fail if individual gifts are stifled beneath a unified, if stagnant, whole.

Religious communities need such directors—neither autocrats of the past nor nonexistent vacuums of the present, but faith-filled, serving leaders of the pilgrim communities of the future.

. 7 .

An Examination of Conscience on the Vows

The older manuals of religious life often featured some type of meditation on the vows, seemingly aimed at giving us great guilt because we were not angels, but all-too-human beings. In a variety of reconciliation services with groups of religious, I developed a set of questions I am inclined to ask myself from time to time, based on the positive, process-like character of the vows. They produce their own kind of shame, but one that moves me forward rather than grinds me further down. It may help to reflect on these questions, to pray for healing where necessary, and to remember that the same God who calls is the God who makes it possible for us to accept and to live out the call.

Premise:

Our religious vows are meant to free us to love and to serve people, to build the kingdom of Jesus' Father, a kingdom of justice, of love, and of peace.

1. Poverty:

By my vow of poverty am I really free not to possess things? Free to share everything with any who are in need, not just within my own community?

Does poverty free me to open my doors, physical and psychological, to share of table and time with any who are in need? Am I growing in the ability to share my richest nonpossession, myself?

2. Chastity:

By my vow of chastity am I really free to love?

Or am I afraid of relationships? Do I avoid friendships with men? With women? Do I love people outside my religious and Church community? Is my love only for the saved or is there a special love for the sinner?

Do I hide behind walls to protect this virtue, as if it were an end in itself?

Am I free to move to new places, new works because I have no unbreakable ties with anything or anyone but Jesus? Do I really love, and trust, and remain open in every situation to my sisters or brothers, especially within my community?

3. Obedience:

Obedience ought to free me to respond, in service to God's Spirit; do I experience it that way?

Am I listening to that Spirit, not just in superiors, but in my own heart? In my community? In the Church? In world or neighborhood? Do I read? Watch the news?

Do I question with all my community what we are about? Or am I content to do what I am told, following the law, but, perhaps, not the Spirit?

Am I open to change the way I live or the work I do if love demands it?

4. Composite:

When my life is over, and I and my community stand before God, he will not ask if I kept the rule, prayed, took vows, but he will ask me:

I was hungry all over Seattle (Boise, Toledo, Detroit, Lesotho); did you feed me? I was thirsty; did you give me drink?

I was a stranger in your city (parish, village, community); did you welcome me and take me in?

I was sick, a leper, an unwed mother, an aged sister; did you take care of me?

I had no clothes; was your closet open to me?

I was in prison very near to where you live; did you visit me? I was anyone in your community, your parish, your country, your world, who needed love; did you notice me? Did you notice the structures that helped to make me that way? Or were you following your rule, saying your prayers, protecting your vows, and you walked by?

I say with the centurion, "Lord, I am not worthy . . . speak but the word and I will be healed."

And he speaks; we are healed, and we rise and go on.

. 8 .

Religious Community and the Eucharist

A priest friend of mine who works in the outer parts of Tanzania has developed a unique, insightful appreciation for the Eucharist in its relationship with community. In villages where he can only visit once a month, the day of his presence is Mass day, all day. His people gather at the Church in the early morning. A brief ceremony sets a tone for the day, and the people disperse to go about their ordinary lives, preparing throughout the day for an afternoon liturgy. Just before they leave in the morning, the priest plucks a clump of grass and hands it to one person. Throughout the day the grass passes from person to person as they meet on a road, in a field, or in front of one another's homes. The grass, a living thing, symbolizes peace, and if one is not at peace with another he cannot pass or receive the grass. The community regroups in the afternoon to celebrate the Eucharist only if the grass has passed successfully throughout the day. If not, they do not have Mass because the grass did not pass.

This priest has had occasions on which, for example, a father and son were not speaking to each other, so they could not in honesty pass the community's sign of peace between them. Once, for a period of three months the entire community

44

went without the Eucharist because of this father-son split. Imagine the difficulties within any religious community that dared to utilize such a symbol. How sad, yet how instructive about our celebrations of the Eucharist. More sadly still, most of us would not even think of such symbolism because we have lost an appreciation for the integral connection between a community and the Eucharist which is a sign of and means towards that community.

I would like to refresh our memories about St. Paul's teaching throughout 1 Corinthians, especially 11:27–29. Listen to it:

> Whoever, therefore, eats the bread or drinks the cup of the Lord in an unworthy manner will be guilty of profaning the body and blood of the Lord. Let a man examine himself, and so eat of the bread and drink of the cup. For any one who eats and drinks without discerning the body eats and drinks judgement upon himself.

Read out of context this challenging passage could lead anyone to question his unworthiness and perhaps never approach the altar. If we wait to be worthy of God's intimate love for us in Jesus, we would never go to Communion. But Paul has a very specific kind of unworthiness in mind, one which challenges our perception of this sacramental gathering as much as it challenged those early Corinthians.

The entire letter to the Church of Corinth concerns unity within the Church. These early Christians, in perhaps the roughest town of Greece, missed the point of the presence of Jesus among them. They boasted about their charismatic gifts and about their origins as Christians. Some were proud to be from Paul, some from Peter, some from Apollo. Paul reminds them that they are all from Christ. Then, for most of the letter, Paul calls them to unity, eventually, in chapter 12, the unity of the body, in which every member depends on every other member to be themselves. This body is the Body of Christ.

Just before the passage quoted above, Paul laments that their lack of unity shows itself even (especially) when they come together for meetings, for remembering the Lord, for Eucharist. The sacred meal, following a sort of potluck dinner, intended to bring diverse people together, but degenerated to a totally opposite symbol. Some brought meat, some fruit, some wine, and some, poorer among them, brought nothing at all. At this meal in the early Corinthian Church the same things happened that occur in any school cafeteria or parents' gathering today. People broke into small cliques, groups of friends, closed, separate. Each ate his own food, some drank too much wine, without sharing any of it, and some went hungry, even in the midst of their so-called Christian friends.

If we understand this context, then go back and read Paul's line about eating and drinking unworthily. We begin to see his point. He says it quite specifically: ". . . in an unworthy manner will be guilty of profaning the body and blood of the Lord." What is this Body of Christ? The consecrated bit of bread? The community that shares of that bread? Both? Yes! Paul means very seriously, and so should we, that if we eat the Body of Christ from the altar without paying attention to the Body of Christ in the pews or chairs around us, we trifle with the death of Christ. We are called to be formed into what we receive. If we refuse to recognize that connection, we are not serious about the sacrament we are receiving, and, effectively, eat and drink a judgement about ourselves.

It is astounding that a parish community, a religious community, any community can share at the same table, listen to the same word, celebrate the same redemptive reality, and not be, as individuals, closer to each other after a few weeks, or even years, than they were before. We have to question with Paul the very validity of that worship that does not transform lives, transform groups into communities.

Transformation does not happen magically, supernaturally, as we are overwhelmed by God's grace, unless we know what the sacrament means and open ourselves to that transformation.

We have used the word "grace" so long that it has become almost emptied of its content. It sounds like a thing, some spiritual aspirin tablet or Elmer's glue. We too often think of grace as something that comes automatically when we perform the proper actions, pour water on the head of an infant or stand before a priest to proclaim marriage vows. But grace is a much more dynamic word and concept than that. It means gift, the gift of God, given not because we earned it, deserved it, but because he loves us. Most importantly, it is not a thing at all; it is a person. The gift of God is Jesus Christ. To grow in grace is to grow in a loving relationship with the person Jesus and to gradually become more like the beloved. The grace of the Eucharist lets Jesus love us into becoming his presence in the world, so that now we live, no longer ourselves, but Christ lives in us. We become the one whom we receive, transformed by this gift, this person, Jesus.

The Jews had a very simple but accurate idea of physiology. A person was alive when he had blood in veins, flesh on bones. In death, the blood coagulates, the flesh slips off the skeleton. To have flesh and blood is to be alive. Jesus did not propose cannibalism ("Eat my arms and legs. . . ."), but a more incredible idea still: that we eat his flesh, drink his blood, that is, assume his very life into our life, let him live in us. The gift of the Eucharist is the gift of Jesus' life in ours, so that his blood flows in our veins, his flesh is on our bones. More concretely, through this continued celebration, we gradually learn to love the way Jesus did, everyone, everywhere, to the point of death. Obviously, the gift implies a commitment also . . . to receive Jesus is to pledge to love each other the way he loves us or to become, in the language we have been using from Paul, his body, still living in the world.

The intimate connection between community and Eucharist becomes clear in this light. The most important words of the celebration seem no longer "This is my body . . . my blood," or "Lord, I am not worthy . . . ," but "The Mass is ended, go to love and serve the Lord." The way we live out the gift is the only indication we have of whether or not the gift was actively received. The way we become the living presence of Jesus in the communities in which we find ourselves fleshes out the symbol we celebrate. Our ability to recognize the Body of Christ in his Church, or any part of that Church, real or potential, is directly proportionate to and dependent on our ability to recognize the Body of Christ in a small piece of bread. We are invited to say "Amen" to each.

How sad then to see communities of sisters, a pastoral team of priests, any "religious" community claiming to center its life around the altar of the Lord, not becoming, through this centering, an amazingly loving group of people. What is the sister doing who goes to Mass every day, often with the people she lives with, when she does not speak to another sister for days on end or has refused to really love and accept that sister in other, more subtle ways? If the grass does not pass, we should not have Mass.

Louis Evely points out somewhere that Jesus spent three years forming a community and only said one Mass. That little quip challenges us to make our Eucharist constantly more valid in its perceived and lived-out connection with our lives. When liturgy becomes ritual, a duty, a magically saving event, we cheapen our richest possession and risk judgement because we trifle with the death of Christ.

I have focused on the act of Communion, but that reception of the Body of Christ is part of an entire ceremony, and each of the parts is important. They need to become more genuine, more honest within each community for the sacrament to truly witness and move us to witness to Christ's being alive among and within us. A religious community that gathers around the altar, gathers and is formed around every part of the action that transpires at that altar.

Imagine a community of sisters, big or small, who regularly celebrate the penance rite with which the Eucharist begins, not with a formula, the recitation of the Confiteor, or a Lord-have-mercy litany, but with an honest admission of faults and sincere begging for healing. We can be very critical of the faults of others until we appreciate that they are critical of the same faults within themselves, that they see their sin and ask the Lord to change them, admitting to us their need for change. A community of sinners is a Christian community for it shares its need for a redeemer as well as its faith that the redeemer is at hand. A community that regularly prays together for corporate and individual healing has already gone a long way towards becoming a Eucharistic community.

In any relationship, dialogue precedes union. Too often in liturgy the proclamation of the word becomes only a hurried preamble to a then artificial and superficial Communion rite. The Eucharistic community each day ought to be formed by the Word of God, challenged into being the community bound up in that one bread, one cup. A community of religious, regularly celebrating the Eucharist together, will be changed in some proportion to the seriousness with which they listen and respond to the readings of the day.

The Church indicates the need for at least a brief homily even at daily Masses. The presumption, too often indeed presumptuous, is that the celebrant knows the community and can indicate the links between this word and this community with some application to their ongoing life. When those elements are not present, if the Eucharist is to be at all what it is intended to be, the community has to seek out other ways to let the word form them.

A community could well meet for fifteen minutes before the Eucharist, listening to that word, reflecting on its meaning for this community this day, perhaps searching for a form of shared homily within the group. However it is done, if a community gathers around the altar, it first wants to gather around the word. It is almost inconceivable that a group of Christians would not find themselves transformed if the gospel spoke personally to them each day or several times each week. Too often we have let that word be heard in utmost passivity as if it spoke to some other group, somewhere else. If it speaks to us, it both challenges us to change and provides the means to live out that change. The challenge to any community, perhaps particularly to that community that lives together, witnessing to the life of Jesus, clearly becomes: How do we make this Word of God a living Word, inviting us to live this gospel, through this Eucharist, today.

The prayer of the faithful can be either a rote listing of objective petitions or the shared hopes of this very real group. I have seen communities who use this part of the Eucharist to express their personal and communal confidence in God and the elements that seem to stifle or challenge that hope today. The relationships between the members of this gathered community grow as, in faith, their needs are placed in the Lord's hand . . . this sister's health, that sister's struggles with a love relationship, another's dissatisfaction with a job, or frustration with the consumerism or militarism of the world she is caught up in. The honest opening out of each member's struggle binds the group more closely into the pilgrim people it calls itself. The quality of those few moments of shared prayer provides enormous potential for the quality of the rest of their lives together within community.

The Eucharist, as its name implies, primarily invites Christians to be thankful. A group authentically celebrating God's love for them with regularity cannot help but grow in knowing how blessed it is, how loved by the Lord. To continue to hope together, the blessings of this day, week, year, must be spoken. I recommend to any community small enough to do so that the preface to the Eucharistic prayer be the sincere thanks of these people, the voicing of what they are grateful for right now around this altar. Let us share that and build each other up in our so deeply needed sense of being blessed.

Each of the above suggestions, and any number of possible ones, will emerge of themselves from a group serious about the "Body of Christ" dimension of their sacramental prayer. The challenge not to trifle with the death of Christ looms ominous to many of us if the divorce between liturgy and life remains. It does not have to remain.

A final word: I recall vividly the awkwardness with which the kiss of peace was introduced in many communities. It seemed so artificial to turn to greet a more-or-less stranger who accidentally neighbored me in church or chapel. Often, little in the preceding moments of Mass called us to recognize those sinners-now-saved listening to the word with us, praying alongside us, about to enter more fully into us and the Lord in Communion. Unless the Mass itself, in each of its parts, calls for lateral as well as vertical worship, the greeting of peace *is* artificial. But if the entire service is experienced for what it is, the most natural, even essential, thing imaginable would be to turn to the Body of Christ found beside me before receiving the Body of Christ from the altar. Put another way, the internal experienced importance of the greeting of peace before Communion (or at another appropriate moment) is the best indication I know of how close we are approximating the effort to "worthiness" that Paul speaks of in 1 Corinthians.

Again, the final words remind us what all the others imported: "Go, now, in peace, to love and serve the Lord." Go to live with and to love each other, to be for the world, the still alive Body of Christ.

. *9* .

Religious Life and Freedom

Freedom has become a key issue in every area of Church life today. Religious life is no exception. Though a key area of concern in the gospel and necessary to the entire project of Christian life, freedom cannot be talked about without misunderstanding, or used without misuse. I want to suggest that, as Jesus invites us to take his yoke upon us, part of that yoke is freedom. His freedom is not just a luxury to be enjoyed, but a burden to be borne, a burden that can be light, easy, as he promised.

I can begin to illustrate this by telling an old story. As all good stories, this one begins "Once upon a time. . . ." Once upon a time a young woman wanted to be a good wife. She was not deeply in love, but a fine young man had asked her to marry him. She was twenty-five years old, mature, sensible, and had seen her vocation to be all that a wife should be. Her new husband was very good about helping her to be that excellent wife she so ardently desired to be. He even drew up a list to assist her in that undertaking. The list was very complete. It told her to rise at 6:30 a.m., have his coffee ready by 7:00, to kiss him as he went out the door to work. It dealt with the details of her life—not cashing checks unless there was money in the bank, checking tomatoes in the market to be sure they were not squishy, calling him before he came home from work to see if there were anything he wanted or needed, and other similarly helpful items. And she followed them well. She was a good wife. For several years she did all she could to be the wife she felt called to be. Even her husband would admit, when asked, what a fine wife she was in everything he had required. But she was never really happy.

Well, the husband died (and went to heaven, of course). After a few years the woman met another man who loved her very much. She fell deeply in love and married again. She hardly remembered her earnest desire to be a good wife in the first marriage and simply lived and loved her husband, basking in his deeply felt love for her. She was now very happy, and the days of her former marriage seemed a distant, unreal, now even ugly time.

One day, as she was cleaning out a storeroom in their home, she looked in a book and discovered the list her first husband had so thoughtfully prepared to show her how to be a good wife. She broke out into perspiration, felt weak, confused; she recalled all the pain and effort of those years. She was tempted not even to look at that old list again. Finally, curiosity overcame fear, and she looked . . . and she was amazed. What do you think she discovered?

Well, obviously, she was doing all the same things in this second marriage that she had been ordered to do in the first. She got up about the same time, followed basically the same regime, kept the same rules, but because she was deeply in love, she never thought about it any more. What she had done for years because she felt she had to, she did now because she wanted to in the deepest core of her being.

The story speaks for itself. The woman represents two stages of covenant, two levels of relationship between people, or vis-à-vis God, two ways of being—acting on external ought or internal desire. Adult Christianity and religious life ought to be based on the second type of relationship. Christian freedom means, most simply, falling in love, knowing, first, that we are deeply loved ourselves. It does not mean doing whatever one wants, but rather it means becoming free enough, in love, to love and serve another.

Let me continue a descriptive definition of freedom by looking at Jesus, the perfectly free man, who both knew his Father's love for him and loved others in the freedom that this divine love gave him. Jesus was free but he was not selfish; his loving freedom was quite the opposite of license. Freedom was no easier for him to exercise than it would be for us, and it continually led him to painful choices.

On occasion Jesus had to hurt those he loved the most; witness Luke's version of the finding in the temple (2:41–50) and the pain he caused his father and mother. Jesus faced rejection in the exercise of his freedom. His family and friends did not understand him, even, apparently, feared he was insane (Mk. 3:20–21). He earned the wrath of the Pharisees by showing that people were more important than the Law or the Sabbath, as when he cured the man with the withered hand (Lk. 6:6–11). He found himself the object of scorn and misunderstanding in the house of Simon the Pharisee when he let a prostitute touch him, anoint him (Lk. 7:36ff.). In Mark's Gospel, after the disciples began to recognize that he was the Messiah, Jesus began to tell them of the suffering and death that messiahship would entail, the pain to which his freedom would lead him. He even, angrily, rejected the well-meant, but wrong-headed words of Peter urging him not to suffer ("Get behind me, Satan!" (8:33). He used his freedom to be himself, not who his friends, his family, his Church wanted him to be.

Jesus was free enough not to be overcome by the fear or anxiety he experienced, for fear and anxiety did not rule him. He could choose to go to his passion ("I have a baptism to be baptized with; and how I am constrained until it is accomplished!" Lk. 12:50).

Freedom, for Jesus, meant being who he was and was supposed to become; it meant letting the Father lead him, even to death, knowing that God's love for him would help him to be his deepest self. It was not a freedom to do whatever he wanted, but a freedom to love and serve and to become the Savior.

Freedom, then, is that strange, deep, secure sense of being loved that allows a human being to make good choices, choices to do courageously what one knows God has called him or her to do or be. Freedom is the inner ability to become oneself, able to make choices consistent with one's fundamental call.

The vocation to follow Christ at all, or as a religious man or woman, is a call of the Spirit urging us to the same radical experience of freedom that Jesus had. It is a freedom to be used to continue Christ's own mission of going out to those in need.

Religious vows ought to free us. Religious life lived in community ought to free us. To the extent that our individual or communal life does not make us more free, we want to be renewed or perhaps even to reject what has become an un-Christian lifestyle for us.

While there are many books dealing with the human struggle to be free, I want to suggest one way of looking at and coping with our unfreedoms. Though, ultimately, it is original sin that keeps us from being free, we can put this very generic concept into more manageable form. I suggest that we are not free (as human beings, and as religious men and women) because *we do not know ourselves* (who we are, are called to be), and *we are afraid to find out.*

We do not know ourselves because our "I" is buried beneath so many "we's." We do not easily discover what is uniquely "me." Because we live in all kinds of systems (family, country, Church, religious community, local smaller community, etc.), it is hard for us to discover our own self, our own values, our own personality and vision. Each group of which we are a part, or ever have been a part, gives to us more and more ways of being and doing common to that group: "Our family does it this way. . . ." "As Catholics, we believe. . . ." "The Precious Blood Sisters always. . . ."

No man or woman is an island. We are parts of many systems from birth to death. As Catholics and as members of religious communities we willingly join two more systems that threaten to define us externally in this way. Every community, sub-culture, to which we belong gives us good and/or bad values which we can assume and act on without making them truly our own. Every system presents a "we" that can overcome my "I" with its own goals, modes of operation, habitual ways of seeing things, ingrained attitudes, unquestioned assumptions.

Psychologists, like Harris (*I'm O.K., You're O.K.*) refer to these as "parent tapes," presenting to us values, categories of good or bad that we get from another, externally. They may be good or bad for us, but, initially at least, they are not our values, but a group's, and, to the extent that we are carried by group values, we are not free.

Let me indicate some obvious concrete values a group can (and sometimes does) pass on: Whites are superior to blacks. Good women are differential to men. Good sisters are obedient and always do what they are told. Christians never get angry. Priests are close to God. Chaste people do not have close friends, especially of the opposite sex. Big boys do not cry.

Insofar as we accept, act on, are guided by, things like these, and a million others, we do not know our own "I," and we are not free.

Many "tapes" obviously are good, helpful in training us. My point is simply that, unless internalized and made our own, they inhibit us from being really free. Please do not misunderstand, though. We need guidelines, initially, at least. Rules, directions, habitual patterns of behavior are necessary for us to become adult. Like the Law for Paul, in Galatians, they are the tutors that lead us by the hand to Christ. But when we find Christ and know deeply his love for us, the tutor becomes less important. The list given to guide us is now written in our hearts. The trouble is so often that, even though we have found Christ (or he has found us and we have recognized him), we still have a hard time knowing who we really are before him because our "I" is buried beneath so many "we's."

To a large extent we are (and choose to remain) unfree because we are afraid to discover that "I." It is helpful to admit to ourselves that freedom asks a price. It is in some ways easier to remain part of "we's" bigger, safer than ourselves. Freedom is a risk and every exercise of freedom is risky. It may be more risky not to be free and more damaging to the building of God's kingdom, but we do not always experience it that way. What we experience is how often fear keeps us from being who we are or are called to be.

Though life is centrally about loving, we all experience being afraid to love, unfree, scared of relationships that make demands on us. We fear rejection if we risk caring, fear our motives will be misunderstood and we will be hurt. We are trained, as Catholics and as religious, to fear sexual sins, and perhaps even to shun close, particular friendships. We are afraid of the many ways that pain comes from really caring or being cared about. It is easier to do as the group does, to move with the various crowds of which we are a part, to keep our "I" buried.

Life is also very much about developing the gifts God has given us, letting our peculiar talents be available to Church and world. But it is often easier not to know our talents, to bury them because if we try to use them we may fail. Or, almost worse, we may succeed and be asked to give even more. We may be criticized, rejected, left alone because we are different. So we put some of our best and still unknown self under a variety of bushel baskets and do not let our light shine before men and women.

We are all a little bit like J. Alfred Prufrock, and that is why Eliot's poem is so successful. Prufrock wanted to break out of the patterns he was in, wanted to be less sterile, less predictable. Convention, custom, habit, bound him in, and fear held him back, and he says, sadly, what perhaps all of us have sometimes felt, "I have seen the eternal footman hold my coat and snicker, and, in short, I was afraid." So Prufrock will grow old, hunched, less and less human, more and more faceless at a variety of cocktail parties. The sadness of the poem is the sadness of so many lives that ended far before they ended, where death anticipated the funeral by many years.

To check your own experience and see if what I am saying rings true, I suggest two simple questions for reflection: First, where in religious life do I experience freedom, the ability to really be myself, and how does religious life help me to foster this freedom? Second, where in my religious life do I experience unfreedom, the inability to really be myself, and how does my religious life seem to foster this?

If you were able to respond to those questions with the ambivalence of most religious, you will probably appreciate some reflection on the question: How do we become more free? I want to respond to this in two parts—our freedom as individuals and our freedom within community.

How do we become more free as individuals? In germ, I have already said all I can say. Like the wife in the opening story, we must fall in love. We pray enough to know how deeply loved we are by God. We pray enough to know that we are responding on every level of our life out of a desire to return whatever we can in gratitude for the experience of being loved. That is the entire answer and a lifelong project, but some more concrete suggestions might help.

There is, I believe, a lifetime art of discovering my "I." If I could suggest a primary tool towards that discovery, I would say it lies in developing the ability to question assumptions, any assumptions, any patterns, molds, approaches, that are, or seem to be, inherent in any group I am part of. By questioning assumptions, I grow in my ability to either make conclusions my own or to discard them.

I worked with a community in which all the sisters wore full, traditional religious habits. I was not bothered by their way of dressing, but I was troubled by the unquestioning assumption that this was helping them in their apostolic work. Younger sisters felt it was detrimental to their being truly part of the world around them in a way that would allow them to serve, particularly the poor and the unchurched in their midst. But the community as a whole continued to dress as they had always dressed. Countless arguments could be given for wearing or not wearing the habit. Which is better is relatively unimportant, however strong my personal convictions may be. What is important in terms of Christian freedom, and healthy religious life and witness, is that each sister wearing the habit honestly knows why *she* was wearing it and had made the choice herself. Perhaps she might only be able to choose to dress that way because most of the community wanted it, and she, for a thousand other reasons, wanted to be part of that community—but she did, in some form, choose this mode of dress in freedom. That is what is important.

Every individual religious faces the question constantly of whether to find his or her support in or outside of community. Each individual struggles with that question on their own to some degree. I am troubled by the community that closes off the struggle and makes it almost impossible for its members to have deep and good relationships with "externs." "We find our community within the community"—a dangerous unquestioned assumption. It may not be true for some and, even if true for most, the very fact that it is a forced choice inhibits the honest possibility of deep love in that community, for love is founded on freedom.

I could give countless other examples, but beneath them all would be the encouragement to all of us to question the assumptions of our communities much more than we have done in the past. Our internal freedom and our external mobility to love and serve people is at stake.

I said previously that we do not know very well who we are, and that is why we need to question the assumptions that are inclined to define us too facilely. But I also indicated that we are all a bit afraid to discover that "I," buried beneath defining groups. We need to struggle with that fear. Fear is often the chief temptation preventing Christ from acting in me, through me. Again, I need to continually experience God's love for me, the love that, I am promised, will cast out that fear.

Fear can be overcome in many cases simply by learning to act against it, to move, at least a little, into areas where fear used to stop me. Aristotle was quite right in pointing out so many years ago that we learn a virtue by exercising the acts of that virtue until it becomes a habit. It sounds simplistic, but the fact is that many of us, experiencing fear, simply let the fear run our lives. I am afraid of women, so I do not talk to them—instead of learning to talk to them in gradual stages. I am afraid to go into the neighborhood, to people's homes to visit them, so I stay home and prepare my third grade lessons —instead of picking a few easy homes and moving into such visits gradually. I am afraid of people who are dying, or of a different color, or part of some counter-culture. Do I let that fear determine my behavior? I do not have to.

Only Jesus was perfectly free. Only Jesus knew perfectly well who he was and overcame any fear that kept him from being his unique self. The rest of us approximate his freedom, his conquering of fear. We need much support to do so. That is why some of us join religious communities, in the hope that the group will not inhibit us, but free us to be more Christian, more ourselves, the unique, valuable, lovable person that God saves, calls, challenges to help him create a world more human and more divine.

I want to end these reflections on freedom in religious life by suggesting a series of questions regarding our community, and, specifically, its prayer life as an aid to the continued experience of the God that frees us. We need each other, and we need each other on the level of faith to become the people God invites us to be.

I could write at length, but, in the light of a million books on prayer, will presume that we have some idea that prayer, private and personal, ought to be helping us to "fall in love" with the Lord, and, hence, become more free. If prayer is not doing that over a period of time, I wonder why we keep praying, and what it is we are doing when we pray. The Lord wants us to be like that wife in her second marriage. But let me reflect, through questions, on our communal life as an aid to experience the freeing power of prayer, of God.

Does our liturgical prayer within a community become a freeing experience, a way of meeting the Lord and my community that frees me to love and serve? Do we become progressively aware that I, and my community, are all sinners, deeply loved by God—that I am not alone, the only one who is weak and frail? Do I experience through the initial part of Mass that we are a pilgrim people, finding strength and freedom in our shared weakness? If not, how can we as community celebrate that part of the Eucharist differently to help us?

Is the Word of God alive in our Eucharist? Is it heard together, responded to together, forming us into a people, freeing us to be together who we are? If not, how can we improve this by some communal preparation for the Eucharist, by encouraging the priest to work with *this* community, by some form of shared homily, or by some previous discussion to let that word form and free us?

As we offer ourselves individually and together in the Eucharist do we grow in knowing the hopes, needs, fears, of this community? Am I growing in the ability to voice my own hopes and fears with them, that is, to become more free to be myself before God and my brothers or my sisters? If not, what is the point of our petitions, our moments of prayer, within the Eucharist, and how can we improve them?

Most importantly, are we really becoming a Eucharistic people and not just going to Church together? Are we more and more a thankful people reminding ourselves of how deeply we are loved individually and together so that we cannot help becoming more free to love and serve? If that is not happening, we need to look at this form of prayer which has become, perhaps, mere ritual or the mere fulfilling of the law itself. Attendance at Mass, weekly or daily, can be yet another unquestioned assumption, and can inhibit freedom by being a result of habit more than conviction. A community can pray the Eucharist in ways that truly help it to become free. Am I? Are we?

I am convinced that the renewed rite of reconciliation in

the Church, especially in its communal form, can be an enormous aid to the renewal of religious life, for we live in closer communities than most and need to experience our common healing deeply and often. Do I individually experience this sacrament as guilt producing or guilt allaying—not as a burden, but as an experience that I am more free, less paralyzed, more able to walk in whole new ways? More importantly, are there ways to experience this together, to grow close in common sinfulness and common being-loved-anyway that could give a corporate strength and courage, a deeper sense of freedom? Could my community have reconciliation services five or six times a year, with or without a priest, that would help us really become open, honest, healed before the Lord and each other?

Do our other community prayer experiences honestly seem to be prayer, that is, the shared experience of the Lord loving us? Or have they become straitjackets of routine and boredom? How can our prayer, sometimes at least, honestly express where this community is in fear and freedom? Does common Office, or the Rosary, or even grace before meals, or any other group experience do this? If not, how could they? And if we do not pray together at all, why not and why are we living together at all?

We can help each other to experience the freeing power of prayer not just in this or that prayer form, but in the entire style of our lives together. Does the way we live and work together constantly flow into and out of our prayer? Can we live in such a way that faith and freedom, as significant dimensions of our lives, are not just implicitly assumed, but consciously expressed?

Could we, for example, start any year or period of our lives together with two or three days of shared prayer, perhaps sharing our life of faith with one another, telling the story of our journey with God to those who will share the next stage of that journey?

Could we run any meetings within a religious community, not like General Motors or a local school board, but in a setting of shared faith, initiating any discussion with prayer, speaking from prayer, listening prayerfully to every member of our group?

Can we end even simple conversations, recreations, anything we do together with a moment of simple, honest prayer?

There is a deep challenge to us individually to be constantly more free in the Lord. As people bonded together to share religious lives, we can do so much more than we have in the past to call each other to deeper lives of faith and richer freedom. True, we have all been "burned" by too much structure, too much saying of prayers, too much "common life," but in discarding past forms we have often failed to replace them with deeper, faith-filled, freeing interaction that gives reason to our being together.

We are all trying to become like the wife in her second marriage—loving, serving, laying down our lives, out of internal, deeply felt conviction of the Lord's love. It is neither easy to be free or to grow in freedom, but the struggle is worth what it entails because only if we see our project this way are we moving towards what we claim to be—religious men and women serving the Church and all those others whom Christ came to free.

. *10* .

Religious Life and the Cross

I was extremely fortunate to spend from June 1977 to February 1978 working with a variety of religious communities in Lesotho, a small, independent, black country in Southern Africa. Among other blessings I gained a perspective on religious life as lived throughout the world, as many of the same questions surfaced there that have harassed renewal among communities everywhere. So often what was called "renewal" was seen, externally, as only change that softened everything held sacred for centuries. The step away from external discipline, the lack of order, downplaying humble submission to authority, the movement from traditional humility—all are sometimes seen as a move away from the center of Christianity, the Cross of Christ.

In an age that stresses freedom of the individual, personal fulfillment, development of human potential, even within religious communities, what happens to the Cross, through which we identify with the salvific work of Jesus? Are we not called, as Paul says, to "complete what is lacking in Christ's afflictions for the sake of his body, that is, the church" (Col. 1:24)? Are we not, with Ignatius in his meditation on the kingdom of Christ, called "to share in his sufferings, so that we can share in his glory"?

I would like to reflect on this question by first asking a crucial question: What were the sufferings of Jesus, the Christ?

I suggest that the first suffering of Christ was to be continually led by the Spirit: "The Spirit of the Lord is upon me. . . . He has sent me. . . ." (Lk. 4:18). Throughout Luke's Gospel Jesus is guided by another to whom he responds in faith. The Spirit leads him to John to be baptized, leads him to the desert to be tempted, leads him finally to Jerusalem to be killed. There is suffering, a cross, in pursuing the lead of another greater than yourself, but in whom you find yourself.

Jesus suffered by leaving his home, his friends, his family, in an exercise of freedom that cut him off from everything and everyone precious to him. He was free and exercised that freedom uniquely, but the freedom cost dearly, deeply.

One of the deepest of human sufferings flows from being misunderstood, no matter how we try to clarify by words or exemplify by our lives our message. Jesus suffered misunderstanding from everyone. Church authorities sought to get rid of him because they missed (or saw too vividly) his message. Civil authorities, with their univocal notion of "king," missed his meaning. Religious people questioned him, "Who can forgive sins but God only?" (Lk. 5:21). His own family, in Mark's Gospel, thought him mad, and tried to bring him home. His closest friends ultimately left him at the crucial moment, after misunderstanding him no matter how long they had been with him. Ultimately one of his best friends betrayed him when he realized his hopes had been misplaced. Jesus was questioned by everyone concerning his associations, his ideas, his lifestyle.

Connected with the suffering of misunderstanding is that of loneliness. Who suffers more than one who steps outside accepted boundaries, speaks new and challenging words to unreceptive ears? The Son of Man had nowhere to lay his head, no settled home, no fixed place that was his. He had nothing strictly his own. The agony scene in the garden is not apart from the tenor of his whole life, "Could you not watch with me one hour?" (Mt. 26:40). Kazantzakis' *The Last Temptation of Christ* suggests that his final temptation was the desire to settle down, to have someone to hold onto. That last temptation may be fiction, but is it mere fiction to know the deepest human suffering is that loneliness felt without anyone to call one's own? Jesus' friends were free friends, "Will you also go away?" (Jn. 6:67). They can if they want to, and, finally, they do.

Jesus suffered in his very empathy with the sufferings of others, both physical and moral. He weeps over a city, the death of a stranger, son of a widowed mother, and over the death of his close friend. He is eager to heal ("I do want to . . . be clean"—Lk. 5:13), and in Mark's Gospel he heals despite his own best interests not to—hence the messianic secret. He hurts because others hurt, and he will not turn away from them or let them turn from him in their pain.

Finally, in this light, Jesus, as human, suffers that excruciating uncertainty about the whole direction of his life and work. Anthony Padavano in *Dawn Without Darkness* captures this so well in his meditation "What do you say from a cross." He presents Jesus reflecting on his life, wondering if he did it right, spoke too harshly or too softly, made too few demands or too many; he wonders why his friends have gone away, why he is so alone, why he is dying. At least one gospel suggests that feeling of failure, of abandonment: "My God, my God, why hast thou forsaken me?" (Mt. 27:46). To be human is to suffer doubt, even in the crunch moments of our life, perhaps especially in those moments.

In all these modes of suffering, and many, many more, spread throughout his life as presented in the gospels, and not only on the Cross, the message of Jesus is that suffering done in love and for love is redemptive. In outline form, such suffering is what he accepts and embraces. Religious life is a call to imitate *the suffering of Jesus*, not just any old suffering. The very core of religious life calls one to the kind of suffering indicated by the suffering of Jesus, but that is a suffering we have too easily avoided in some past forms by substituting crosses of our own, arbitrary crosses, not necessarily fashioned in love.

The vow of poverty calls a religious to a free sharing of everything she is, or has, or does . . . with nothing to call one's own. The vow of chastity calls one to love in an unpossessive, unmanipulative, freeing way . . . to really love and yet have no one to call one's own. The vow of obedience calls one to wholehearted service of the kingdom, responding prayerfully to the Spirit of God moving in one's life . . . to become most oneself by answering to another.

Clearly, a positive, humanly developing, Christian understanding of our religious vows opens us to a far greater suffering, a deeper identification with Jesus than was ever asked in a formal or negative understanding. There is a suffering, of sorts, in not personally owning anything, in sharing all in common with a community . . . but it is nothing like the suffering of sharing all of *myself* with everyone. There is hardship in never sleeping with anyone else, but it does not compare to the deeply Christian suffering involved in really loving as widely and deeply as one can, without possessing another or having any claim over them. There is a very real (perhaps unchristian and inhuman) suffering in doing what another tells us. Such suffering is not as deep as the demand made by really praying, being open with my community, listening to the world around me, being honest with myself, and, then, honestly choosing to follow where I think the Lord is calling me . . . and accepting the responsibility for that choice.

Let me spell out the above and look at suffering and religious life as it affects a positive orientation towards sharing in the salvific mission of Jesus. Too often in years past we had a clear idea of what we were against, what we left behind, what we rejected. And there was undoubtedly some pain in this, for often we stepped *away* from parts of a world we had lived in with relative happiness. But today, the Cross of Jesus calls us to stand *for* something . . . to be for the poor, the most needy, to be for love, wherever it happens, and justice, even in our own neighborhood, even to voicing unpopular opinions and standing by them. The suffering in an embarrassing and ambiguous picket line is far more Christian, far deeper, far closer to the gospel than the pain of asking permission to buy a ballpoint pen.

We used to envision religious life as transcending the world, and there was pain in stepping aside "out of the swing of the sea." But it is a so much more Jesus-like suffering to love that world, to transform that world, to be immersed in that world, to be buried by that world, hurt by it, saving it. We used to speak of vowed lives of faith, but now we are called to the active faith that does justice, a constitutive element of the gospels.

I am suggesting then, that there is unavoidably greater suffering in religious life today, and that religious life can provide, in fact must provide, in huge measure, the opportunity for the kind of suffering that is redemptive.

Further, since there is enough suffering provided by trying to be a loving presence of Jesus in the world, we badly need to relieve religious life of all the artificial suffering it has cluttered itself with the past hundred years or more—the petty permissions, the humiliating corrections, the rigid rules, the execution of orders of the day, the restrictions on clothing, travel, entertainment that come from without a person (though many will come from within a religious today), the limiting of visits, and visions, and relationships. Religious must be freed to live the vows they have taken . . . to love, to share, to serve.

To have nothing of one's own, but to share one's time, energy, goods, talents, joys, sorrows. . . .

To have no one of one's own, but to love deeply, always ready to move on to other, greater needs. . . .

To be ready at all times to go where God's Spirit leads. . . .

To live in faith, walking always on stormy waters. . . .

To live in hope, believing in the ultimate good sense of God's promise. . . .

To love with a love overflowing from an ever-deepening experience of God's prior love for me. . . .

Is to open oneself to ultimate, deep, consistent, unavoidable suffering . . . and to a joy that knows no bounds, and never ends.

Epilogue:
Religious Life and Joy

> These things I have spoken to you, that my joy may
> be in you, and that your joy may be full (Jn. 15:11).

When I completed this manuscript I asked a friend to read
it. Though I questioned her objectivity, she did enjoy my
comments but felt cheated at the end. She objected that I had
stressed joy throughout and then ended with the struggles
and the hardships of religious life. Where was the joy? She
said she knew me as a fairly happy man and insisted I should
end by telling why, saying, with Hopkins, "What is all this juice
and all this joy."

So, this chapter, epilogue really, is an effort to respond
to her, and perhaps to anyone else who asks a similar question.
Necessarily I will talk about myself, as if I had not done so
sufficiently already. But I resist the inclination to apologize
for biography at this stage, believing that we are all so much
alike that what I say about myself, if true, will be true of you
also.

I am happy, generally. My life as priest and religious has
much to do with that, but it is difficult to say exactly what.
Much more easily do I speak of death than resurrection.

The message of Jesus is said to be of joy—the hundredfold

his followers reap not only at the end but now (Mt. 19:29). To believe in Jesus is to believe this too, and to experience it also. I do. Perhaps I can begin to tell you something of that experience.

Most significantly, I am happy because I am convinced that God has loved me, loves me now, will love me in whatever future comes. I waver on that often, lose track of God's goodness, because I doubt my own. But deep down lies that "peace that passes understanding," rising from the many, subtle, mysterious moments when God has said his Yes to me, despite my infidelities, imbecilities, inadequacies, fears and foibles beyond anything I thought myself capable of when my religious project was just that—*my* project, not God's.

I am happy, principally then, because I experience myself as sinner, but more importantly as a called, loved, chosen, redeemed sinner. It is all right, I discover, to be a sinner. In fact, there are no other people, only those who mistakenly think so, and they are the saddest people of all. I am a sinner. Jesus came for me, for us. I believe that. It gives me great joy.

I am happy because I find myself becoming poor and chaste, obedient and free, and am enjoying the process.

Nothing makes me more happy than to be led to believe that I have something to give. I love it when people ask me to preach, to teach, or to talk with them about their lives. I used to worry more. "What do I have to say . . . to give . . . to be?" When I preach I talk to myself and let others listen if they want. When I teach I read the poems I like or tell of theological, religious ideas that make sense to me. Hopefully others like them too. When I counsel or give spiritual direction, I talk about myself or rather listen with that other ear that reminds me I am hearing again my story, my hopes, my fears, and I try to let a friend know that he is not alone.

One of my favorite things happens when my friends meet my friends and become friends themselves. I like to have company for dinner, extra people living in my house, prayer with Jesuits and others of my brothers and sisters. This happens often and makes me glad. I get tired and forget, but, basically, I like to share who I am and what I have.

And I am gradually becoming, through no real fault of my own, more celibate and more loving. I remember reading a letter some years ago in a *National Catholic Reporter* in which a priest of fifty-five said he had fallen in love for the first time and had to leave and marry. It made me sad to think of fifty-four years without love, sad to think that, for him, love meant he had to marry. I fall in love a lot, with kids, with elderly people in a parish, with other Jesuits, and, yes, with women friends. It has been painful at times for them and for me. I have made mistakes and hurt people I honestly cared about because I said more than I meant or meant more than I said because I promised more or less than I could live up to. I have held on too tightly, or not tightly enough, have been too distant, and too close. I have wanted to control, and, at times, to let others control me. But God has blessed me with wonderful friends, and they have loved me through my stumblings and raised me up, so often with a smile.

The women who have loved me have been special gifts. By loving me they have led me to know that love of the Lord I speak about, have been sources of perhaps my deepest joy. These relationships have not been without struggle and pain, but no joy comes without these. I am learning to love in return without needing to possess or to control. I honestly believe that what we surrender in depth and extent and intensity in choosing not to marry is enriched by great depth, extent, intensity in many relationships if we are not afraid to let the Lord love us in this way. And I like who I am becoming more than who I have been; this brings me joy.

I am happy because I am beginning to see the connection between prayer and obedience, between listening to God's voice within and around me, and letting that voice lead me, rather than to muddle my own way alone. I am still apt to be led by almost any wind, tend to either join every cause or feel guilty because I do not join. I still find it hard not to just respond inadequately to every voice, but to prioritize and replace quantity with quality. But I am growing, am becoming obedient. There is a joy for me in letting go of the controls and moving with the Spirit that is new and peace giving to me.

So, I am becoming, I believe, more free, free to be the unique me that God intensely loves. There has been pain in that freedom—pain of moving from one job to another, from some relationships to others, pain in keeping friendship alive across new distances. Like Charlie Brown, "Goodbyes make my throat hurt; I need more hellos!" But there grows a deep sense of freedom in every farewell that causes tears because it tells me I was really there, really present, not just doing a job, putting in time, but becoming vulnerable and deep by loving a little more as Jesus did and being free enough to move on as he did too. Each farewell ushers in the new joy-laden meetings of new friends, new challenges.

I do not mean to say that all my life is puzzle-perfect, forming only beautiful, unified pictures from a thousand diverse pieces. What I can say is that joy comes to me from the effort to live out the project, which seems so clearly a gospel project, that I have outlined in these pages.

In a retreat recently my director asked me at the end to write my own version of Ignatius' famous "Suscipe." I struggled a long time and finally wrote it by not writing it. The results say a lot about my joy, the joy of religious life.

Contemplation for Accepting Love
I cannot say, with heart, that prayer,
cannot give away
what never was possessed,
what's his already
so much more than mine.

I'd like to lose my memory,
parts of it;
forget my infidelities, imbecilities,
crimes and cruelties,
loves lost, hurt, helpless.
Such memories are not mine to conjure up,
control, release, remove,

or even learn from.
I pray: Remind me of my gifts,
your love,
all the cliffs I've stood beside,
tottered over,
not fallen.
Help me to recall the lapses
life has left me,
as things I have survived. . . .
Heal my memories, Lord.
My understanding . . .
always more a standing under.
Needed truths hung over my head
as threats,
or shields,
umbrellas from a storm sometimes,
but never mine,
possessed,
to give away, give back.
I do not understand myself,
yourself,
life, luck, love,
sin, sadness, suffering,
cricket scores,
or scores of other things.
I pray: Lord, understand me,
more than I do myself;
Keep smiling,
even when I can't.

Most especially have I never owned
my will.
Bird's freedom, blown by every wind,
frisbee, circling where life's spin
has spun it.
Take my will, and whirl it
where you will,
to give my will to you is whim.
I pray: Handle me with care;
surround my fickle heart

with choices between goods,
let your kingdom come through good intentions
half unfulfilled.

I'm willing to give up
whatever I may have,
or will possess.
It's surely not myself,
but you,
Lord,
can have that too.

Your love I need,
your freely given grace,
Your Son, desired, undeserved,
and dear.

It is in needing everything,
possessing nothing,
that I am rich.
And I am rich!
Possessing only You.

The AUTHOR

Fr. L. Patrick Carroll, S.J., currently is an associate pastor of St. Joseph's Church, Seattle, Washington, and co-director of the Institute for Spiritual Resources in that city. He has taught English and theology classes in Jesuit schools in Washington and Oregon. He has served as a religious superior, and he has done retreat and religious renewal work in the African nation of Lesotho, with priests, sisters, and brothers of that nation, and has trained retreat directors. His previous publications include the co-authorship of *Faith in the Face of Doubt* (Paulist Press, 1968) and articles in *The Priest, Cross and Crown, Ave Maria, The Way,* and *Sisters Today.*

Cover by Br. Placid Stuckenschneider, O.S.B.